Dad

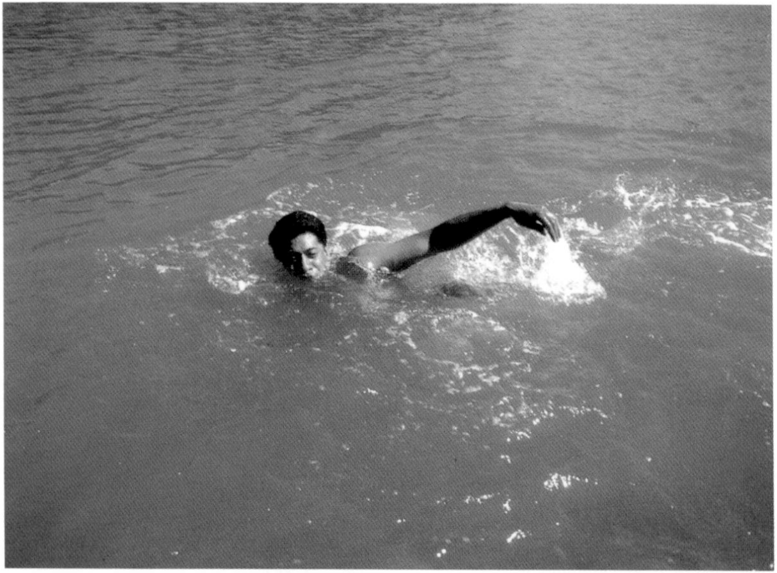

Dad is cooking.

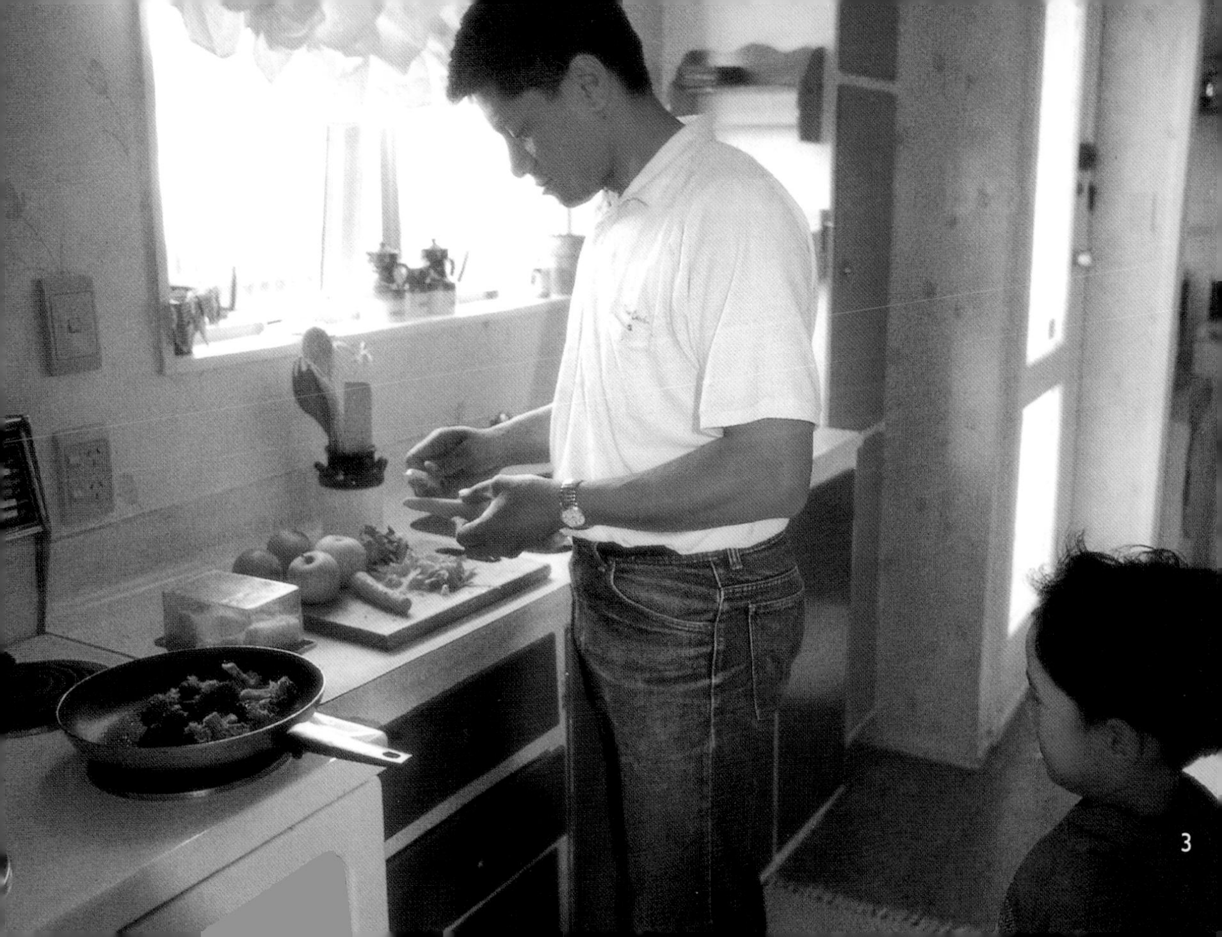

Dad is painting.

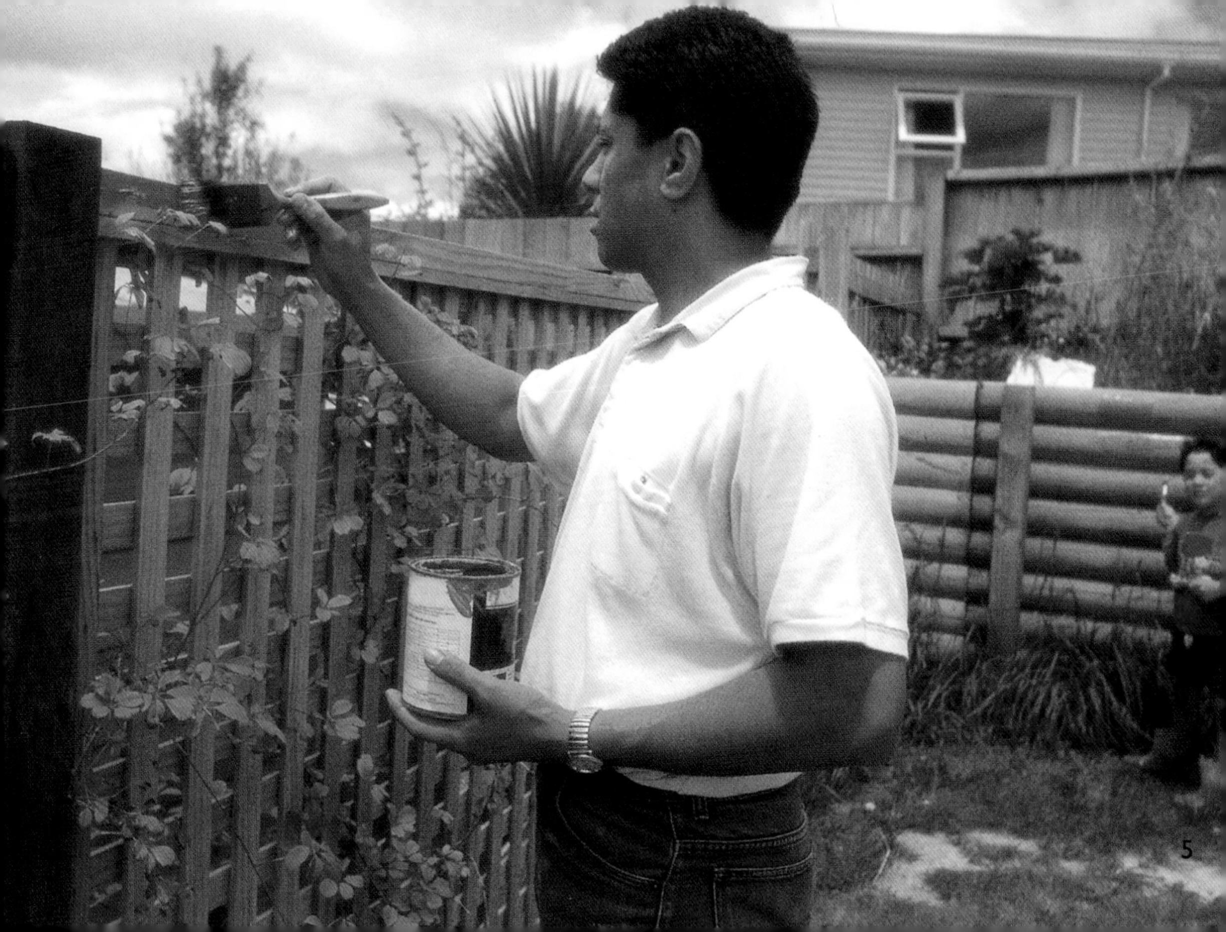

Dad is driving.

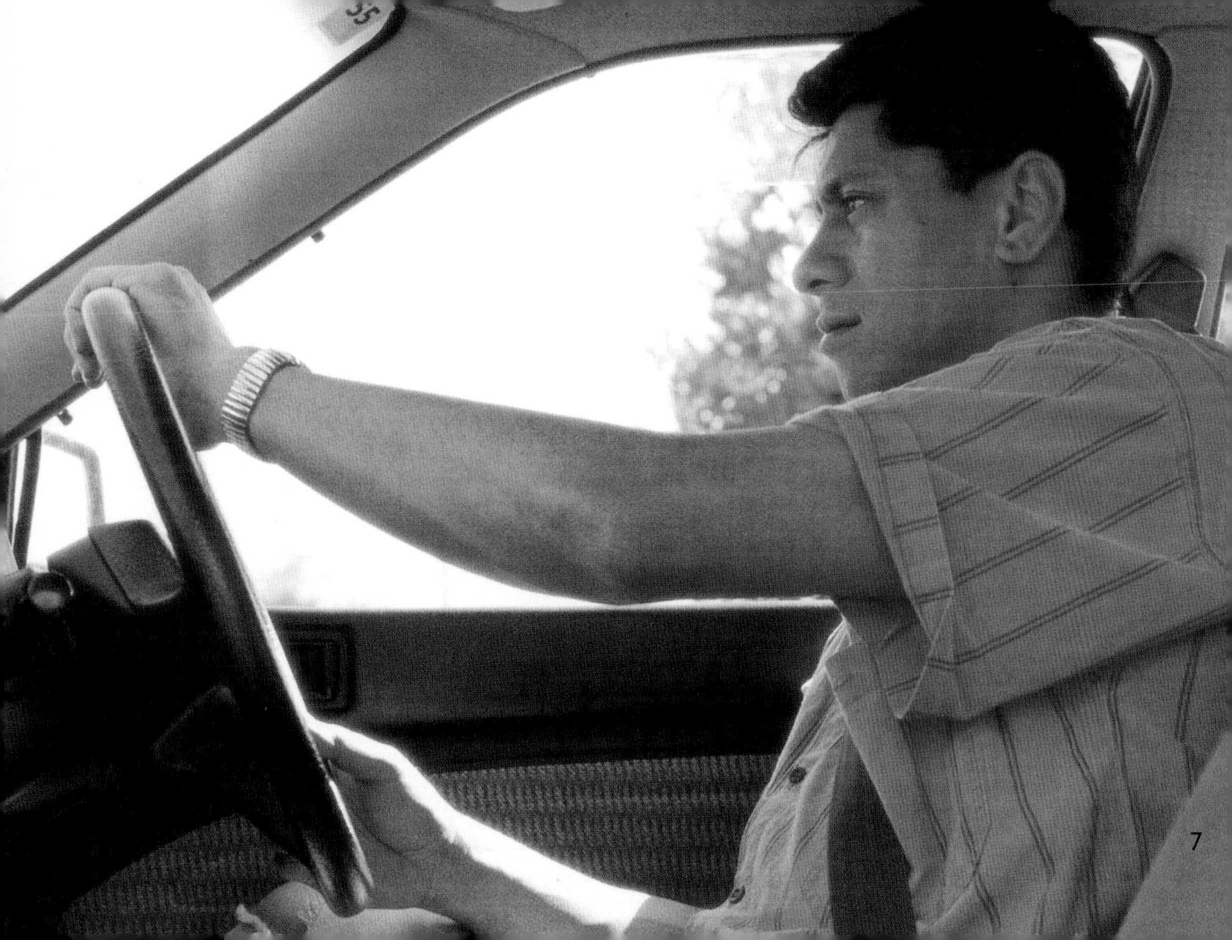

Dad is swimming.

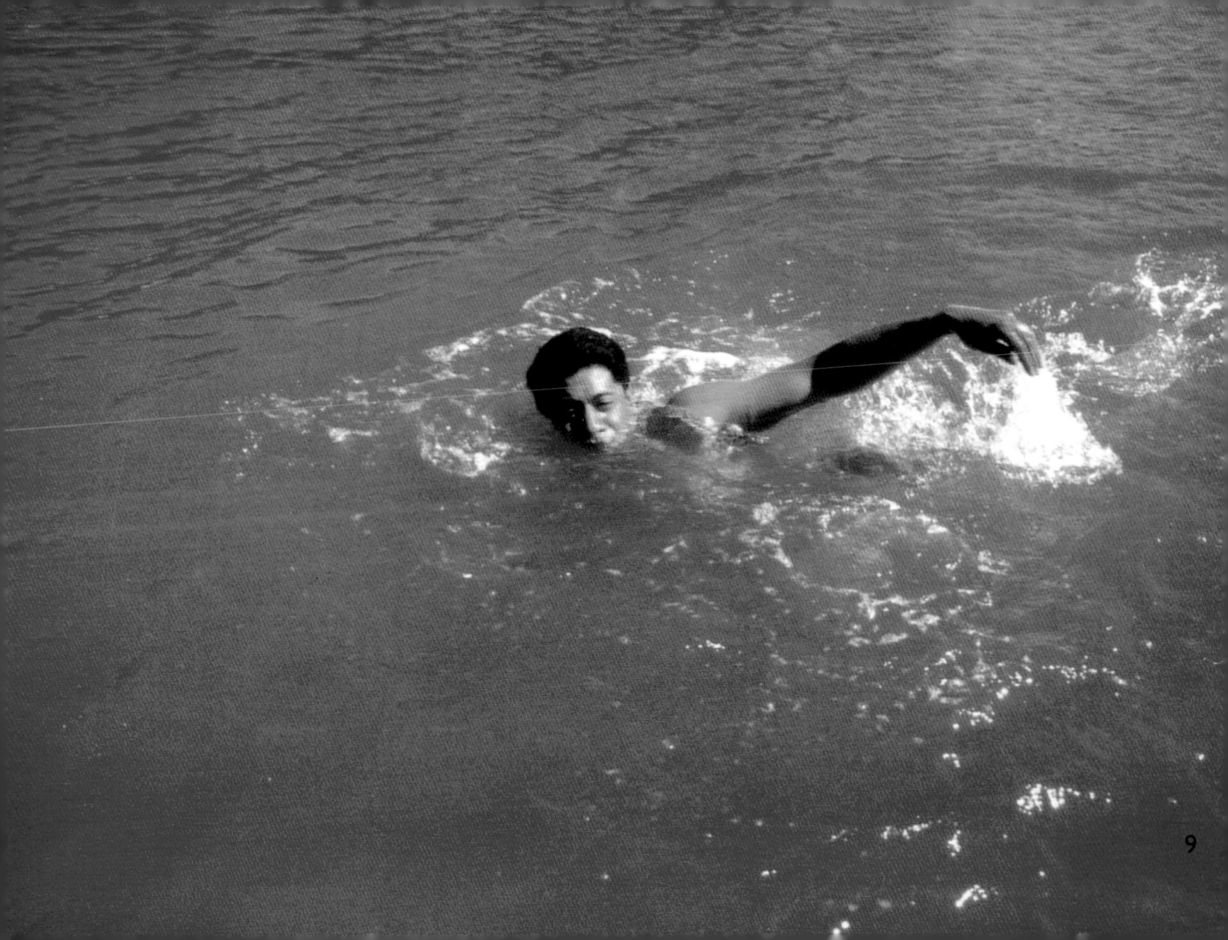

Dad is digging.

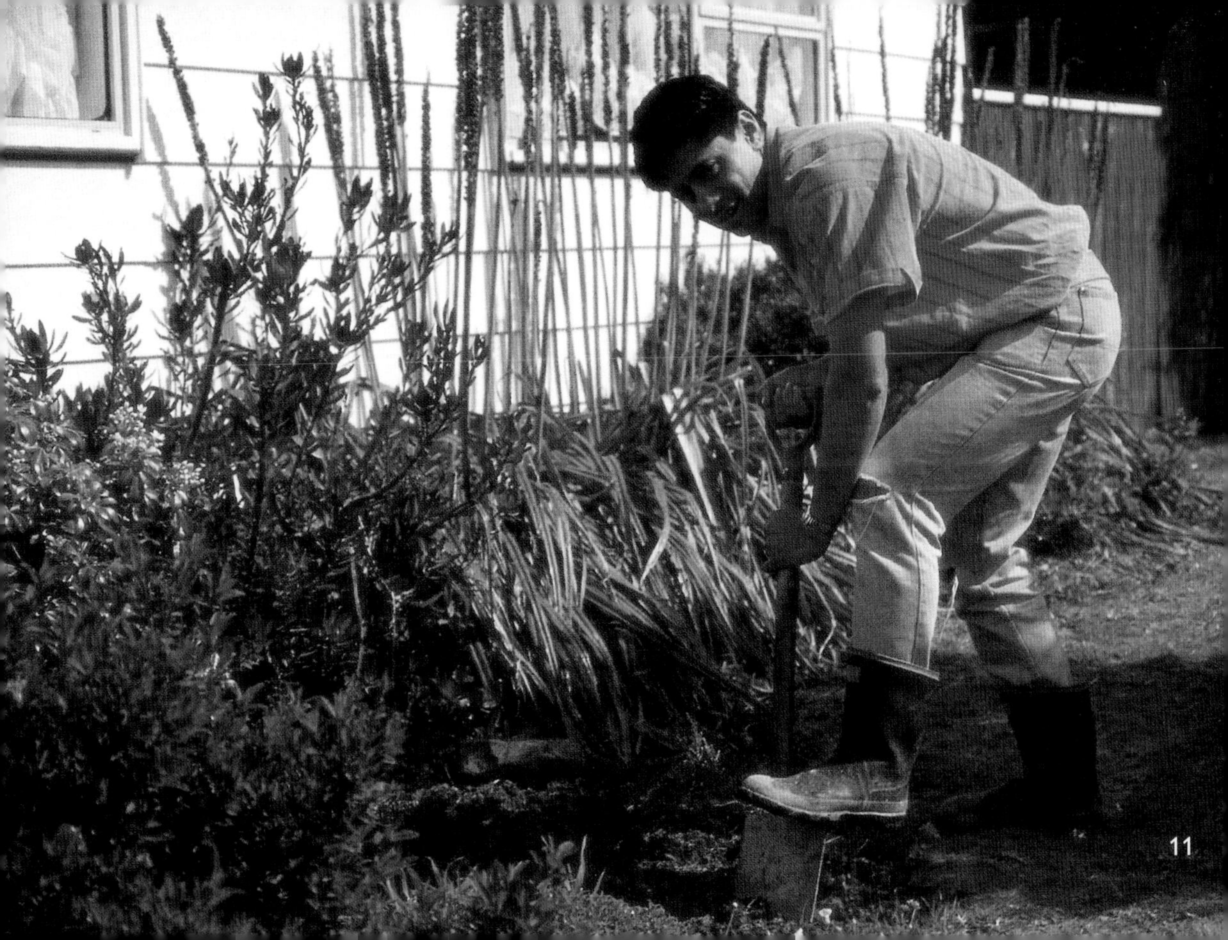

Dad is running.

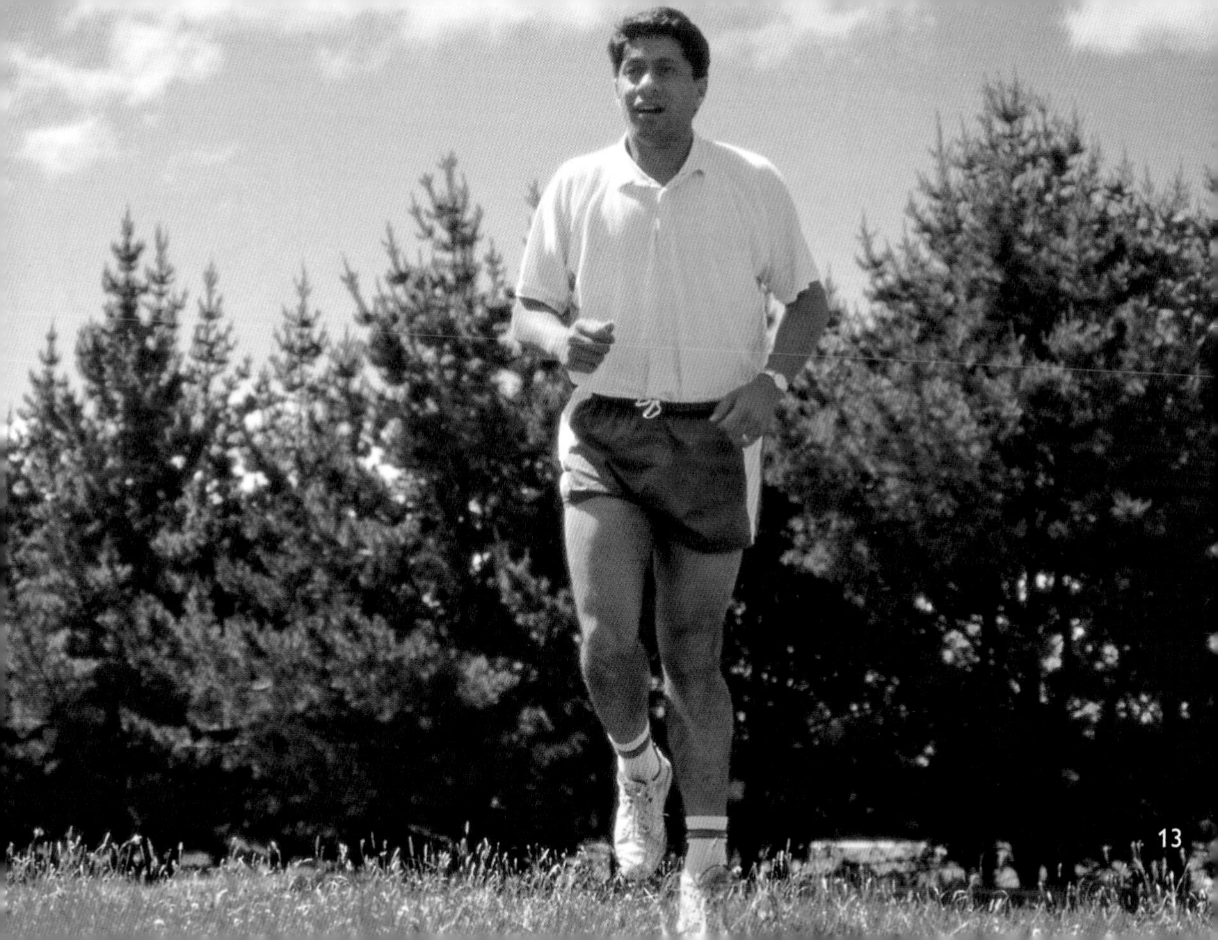

Dad is reading.

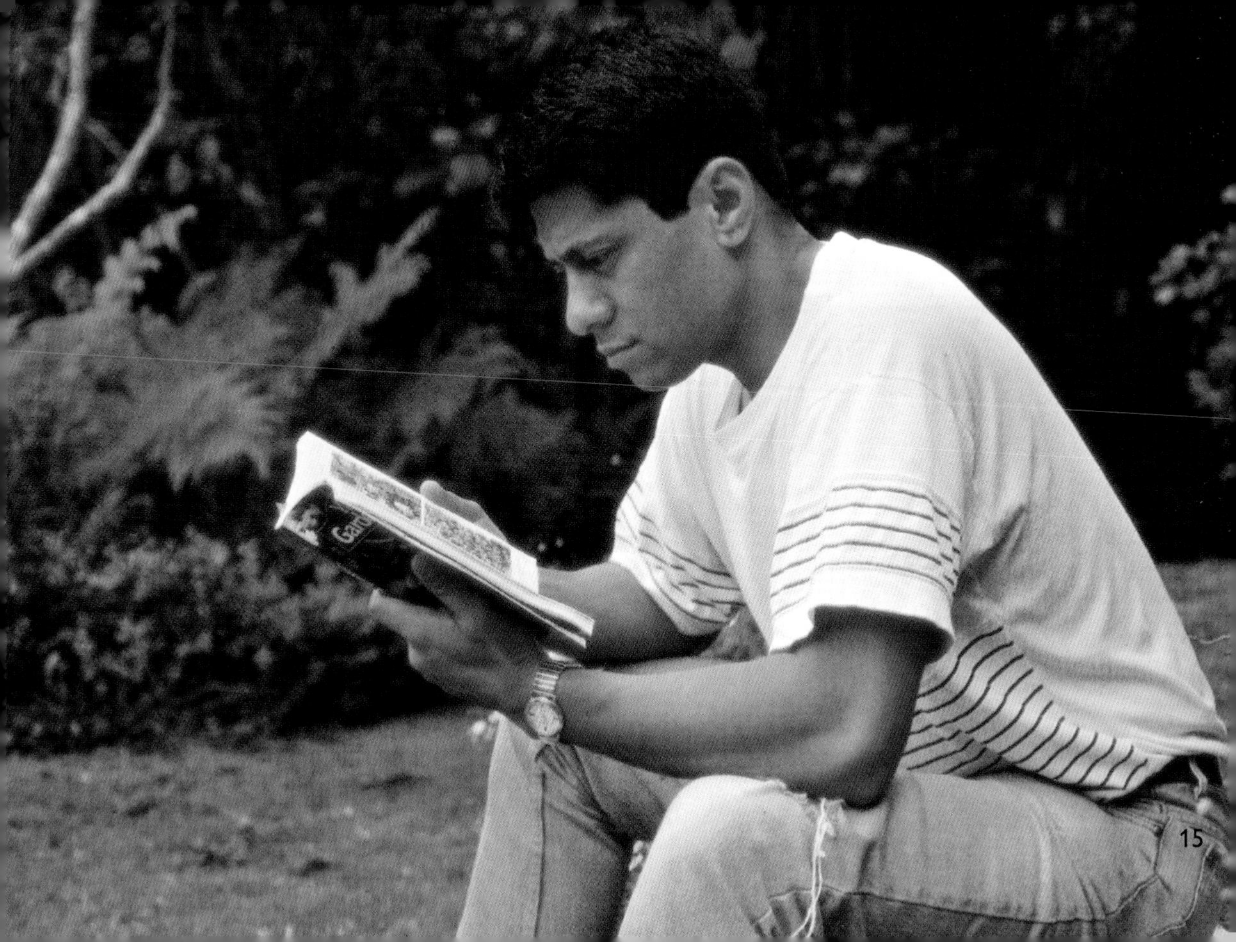

Dad is sleeping.

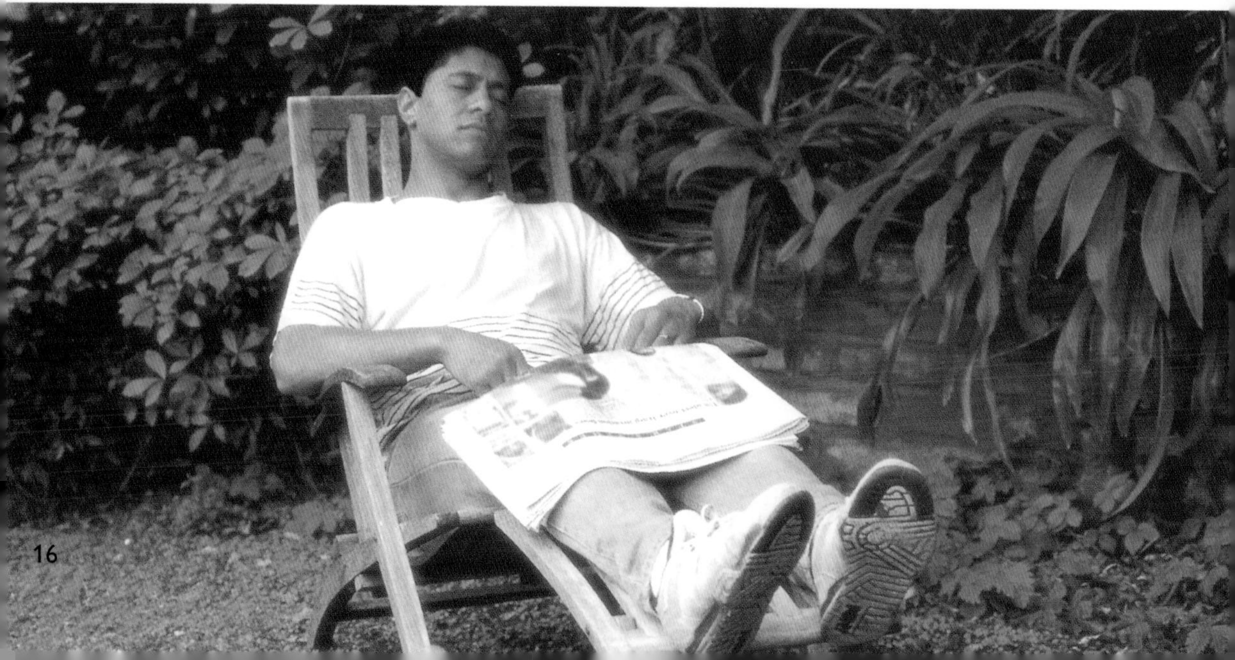